Original title:
Stardust Speakeasy

Copyright © 2025 Creative Arts Management OÜ
All rights reserved.

Author: Isaac Ravenscroft
ISBN HARDBACK: 978-1-80567-805-2
ISBN PAPERBACK: 978-1-80567-926-4

The Last Light Before Dawn

In the bar of the night, where echoes collide,
Cocktails of dreams and laughter abide.
A jukebox of wishes, spinning tunes so bright,
We dance with the shadows, till the morning light.

With cosmic confetti falling from the sky,
We sip on the giggles, as time flutters by.
A toast to the jesters, who twirl and who spin,
In the last light before the day can begin.

A Glint in the Milky Way

Under twinkling lights, we gather and play,
Mixing up jokes like a cosmic café.
With stars as our witnesses, we chuckle and grin,
Each sip is a story, where nonsense begins.

A comet slipped by with a wink and a cheer,
As laughter erupted, we summoned a beer.
Galactic mischief ignites in our souls,
In the Milky Way's bar where the fun never rolls.

Tales of the Astral Encounters

Once met a green guy who danced with a chair,
His moves were so wild, none could help but stare.
He spilled all his secrets with every "whoop!"
In cosmic cantinas, where mischief can stoop.

A tale of a traveler from Mars named Lou,
He mixed up his drinks with a splash of blue goo.
With quirks and delights, his stories spun round,
Underneath the vast void, with laughter profound.

Cosmic Echoes in the Dark

In the still of the night, we share our delight,
Telling ghostly tales, with a dash of moonlight.
Each chuckle an echo that bounces and swirls,
In this cosmic club, we dance like the whirls.

A riddle or two from the stars in the mix,
Their playful banter, a humorous fix.
With whiskey and stardust, our worries take flight,
In the shadows of space, everything feels right.

The Twilight Affair

In a bar where the shadows dance,
The moon winks, giving a glance.
Martinis mixed with a cosmic flair,
Laughter floats in the starlit air.

A cat in a bow tie sips gin,
While aliens play cards, wearing a grin.
The jukebox hums a tune quite queer,
As comets spin round, bringing cheer.

Neon lights flicker, a dazzling sight,
As patrons toast to the endless night.
With jokes like stars, they twinkle bright,
In this odd, delightful twilight flight.

Twilight's Hidden Tapestry

In velvet seats beneath the stars,
Aliens swap tales of quick little cars.
With drinks that bubble, sparkle, and fizz,
They toast to life and the cosmic whiz.

A raccoon with shades tells a tale,
Of a spaceship that got caught in the pail.
While laughter erupts like supernova light,
The night wears on, it's pure delight.

Glittering voices weave the air,
With secrets and giggles laid bare.
In this playful web of night so sweet,
Each cheeky remark feels like a treat.

The Nightly Reverie

Underneath this cosmic dome,
Spirits laugh and feel at home.
A disco ball spins like a dream,
With every twirl, the stars all gleam.

Martian dancers glide and sway,
As jokes fly round like asteroids play.
Applause erupts for each silly prank,
In this whimsical, galactic bank.

Cotton candy clouds float by the bar,
While giggles echo, near and far.
In the festival of bright delight,
Every soul shines through the night.

Galactic Tales and Twinkles

Once upon a twinkling time,
Where critters sip on space-lime.
The mixed drinks spark, a fruity twist,
In this cosmos, you can't resist.

A wizard's spell gone slightly wrong,
Turns a toad into a karaoke song.
With each high note, stars around explode,
Creating laughter on this starlit road.

With cosmic pies that float in air,
And moonlight cakes without a care.
Guests share stories, both wild and funny,
In this galactic spot - oh, isn't it sunny?

The Celestial Gathering

Beneath the twinkling night sky bright,
The stars all gather, oh what a sight!
With laughter that echoes, filled with cheer,
They toast their drinks, a cosmic sphere.

Jupiter, tipsy, spills his brew,
Saturn dances, what a view!
While Mars attempts a drunken sway,
Veering off in a wobbly way.

Venus, giggling, plays the guitar,
Singing songs of a distant star,
As comets crash in a dazzling swirl,
Creating cosmic chaos with a twirl.

Oh, let us join this grand affair,
The universe's party, beyond compare!
With celestial vibes and funny grins,
The night begins where the laughter spins.

Dancing with Meteors

A meteor shower, oh what a spree,
With glittering trails, wild and free!
They swirl and twist, a lively dance,
    Each one hoping for a glance.

Galaxies spin, giggling loud,
As shooting stars form a silly crowd,
One slips on dust, gets stuck in flight,
    Flailing arms - what a sight!

Gravity pulls on the comets' tails,
They trip and tumble, laughter prevails,
With moonbeams shining, oh so bright,
    It's a wacky, cosmic disco night.

As asteroids roll in with a cheer,
They join the fun, spreading joy and beer,
In the grand expanse, where laughter roams,
Space is their stage, the universe their home.

Elixirs from the Expanse

In bottles shaped like stars so grand,
Potions bubble, created by hand,
With flavors that tickle and spark the tongue,
They mix and mingle, oh what fun!

A splash of nebula, a twist of light,
Sipping stardust, feels just right,
Martian margaritas served with a giggle,
Each sip makes you dance and wiggle.

The Milky Way drinks like a fine wine,
Glistening like a cosmic design,
Black holes serve cocktails, dark as night,
Swirling flavors that take you out of sight.

Yet beware of the cosmic schnapps,
One sip and you'll melt like galaxy claps,
With tittering laughter, the cosmos plays,
In this joyful bar of endless days.

Harmonies of the Celestial Spheres

Up in the heavens, melodies rise,
As planets croon beneath the skies,
A cosmic band with stars in tow,
Playing tunes from long ago.

Neptune strums a watery bass,
While Mercury's fast with a dazzling grace,
Together they create a quirky sound,
As laughter fills the space around.

With asteroids clapping, astounded cheer,
This orchestral night, the best of the year,
Their harmony lifts like a comical breeze,
Tickling the stars and rustling the trees.

So dance with the planets, sway to the tune,
Under the bright and jolly moon,
In this concert where fun never ends,
The universe sparkles, and laughter transcends.

Celestial Cocktails

In a bar made of moonbeams, drinks flow,
Starfruit spritzers and cosmic glow.
Aliens dance on tables of light,
Mixing up laughter with hints of delight.

Martians sip stardust-infused gin,
While black holes giggle, it's all in the spin.
Comets come crashing, but no one gets hurt,
Just extra sprinkles of celestial flirt.

Dances with Distant Stars

Planets spin wildly to funky beats,
Galactic guests in their sequined seats.
They twirl and they whirl, what a sight to behold,
Even the sun joins with shoes made of gold.

Asteroids tap dance, sending sparks in the air,
Constellations grin with a sparkle and flair.
They shimmy and shake, oh what cosmic fun,
A universe party that's just begun!

Ethereal Brews

In a café of clouds, they brew up the best,
Coffee from comets, it's better than rest.
Lattes with lightning, a foam made of star,
Every sip tells a tale, adventures afar.

Whispers of fairies float round in the steam,
Baristas of magic, fulfilling your dream.
A sip of this wonder, and soon you will see,
The laughter of constellations is free.

Luminous Conversations

Chatting with aliens over a bright brew,
Exchanging wild secrets, just me and my crew.
They joke 'bout their ships and their glittery hats,
While dogs in space wear well-fitted spats.

Galaxies gossip, their gossip a blast,
Tales of what's coming and what's already past.
With a wink and a nod, reality bends,
In this cosmic pub where the fun never ends.

The Empyrean Escape

Up high where giggles float,
A cosmic clown forgot his coat.
Juggling moons, he slips and falls,
Laughter echoes through the stalls.

With each bounce, a comet dives,
Chasing dreams where humor thrives.
Stars wink as they take a drink,
In the sky, the jokes don't stink.

Galaxies twist in playful spins,
Bubbles burst with silly grins.
Asteroids crash with a silly sound,
In this realm, joy knows no bound.

The night-time dances filled with cheer,
Alien antics draw us near.
In the clouds, we sip delight,
A heavenly space for jesters' flight.

Midnight Among the Orbs

At dusk when planets start to play,
They roll and tumble, come what may.
A jovial moon grins wide and bright,
Tickling stars with pure delight.

Join the planets in their waltz,
As they trip, there's not a fault.
Each one wearing giggle hats,
Bouncing 'round like silly cats.

Meteor showers rain down jokes,
Each burst sends laughter through the blokes.
Twinkling lights, a show so grand,
We chuckle in this cosmic land.

Imagine comets singing tunes,
A spacey band beneath the moons.
In this night, no frown in sight,
Just merry moments of pure delight.

The Playground of Comets

In a yard where gravity bends,
Comets slide and make new friends.
They soar on swings of shooting stars,
Laughing louder than guitars.

Tethered to the joy they seek,
Stars play hide and seek all week.
A nebula hides behind a sun,
Jumping out and making fun.

Galaxies spin on merry-go-rounds,
Cosmic cheers and silly sounds.
With each twist, they let out shrieks,
In this place where laughter peaks.

Fallen debris becomes a slide,
Joyful rides we can't abide.
In the playground, fun ignites,
As space delights in silly nights.

The Enchanted Cosmos

In the cosmos' playful nooks,
Stars read funny, cosmic books.
Galaxies giggle, twist, and turn,
In their light, bright laughter burns.

Black holes hide with cheeky grins,
Chatting as the journey begins.
Asteroids wear their finest ties,
Cracking jokes in whispered sighs.

Nebulas bloom like flowers rare,
Tickling comets in the air.
Each twinkling light a witty pun,
Dancing 'neath the gleeful sun.

In this realm of sparkling dreams,
Life is bursting at the seams.
With every wink from up above,
The heavens laugh, they shine with love.

Echoes in the Milky Night

Underneath the cosmic glow,
Dancing ants in tuxedoes flow,
Whispers of the stars collide,
With giggles in the dark, we ride.

Gravity has lost its game,
As planets play a trick, how lame!
Shooting stars with party hats,
Twirl like over-caffeinated cats.

Chasing comets, sly and bold,
We toast to tales of ages old,
Each twinkle stirs the mischief sweet,
As meteors waltz on light-speed feet.

In the void where no one sleeps,
The universe just giggles, leaps,
For even black holes can take a spin,
Launching laughs from within.

The Constellation's Masquerade

Peek-a-boo behind the stars,
Mercury drives a shiny car,
While Ursa Major shares a joke,
Laughter bubbles, laughter spoke.

A comet dressed in sequined flair,
Glimmers through the brilliant air,
Asteroids dance in silly shoes,
With Twinkle-Toes in cosmic blues.

The Milky Way rolls out the cake,
With frosting made from moonlit flake,
Each slice a burst of cosmic cheer,
As all the galaxies draw near.

Nebulas swirl in whirly-gigs,
While Nova dons its vibrant figs,
In every corner, fun ignites,
A cosmic ball that stars invite.

Glittering Secrets of the Night

In shadows where the starlight beams,
A billion whispers weave their dreams,
Each speck of dust a tale untold,
In sparkling night, watch secrets unfold.

With pirouettes of solar flares,
And cosmic chips in poker chairs,
The cosmos plays a sneaky hand,
As laughter spreads across the land.

Planets juggling with delight,
In the comical, endless night,
Each wobble hides a cheeky grin,
As laughter echoes from within.

Stars wink like friends sharing wine,
While asteroids do the twist and twine,
The universe in laughter dives,
Tracking joy on its silly drives.

When Galaxies Converge

When spiral arms begin to twirl,
And cosmic dust begins to swirl,
The stars collide in playful jest,
As laughter lifts them, feeling blessed.

In playful groves of twinkling spheres,
Each supernova holds back tears,
Of joy that bursts when forces clash,
A party rising with a flash.

Asteroids play hide and seek,
While laughter rings through cosmic peak,
Gravity pulls on friendship's thread,
As comets giggle overhead.

In a collision of distant lights,
Fun erupts through endless nights,
When galaxies meet under a wink,
The universe pauses, takes a drink.

Celestial Dreams in a Glass

A comet's tail in fizzy drink,
Glimmers of joy, oh what to think!
Martini's moons, they twist and swirl,
In cosmic parties, watch them twirl.

Asteroid snacks, a crunchy bite,
Under the glow of neon light.
Cosmic laughter fills the air,
With every sip, we float, beware!

Grab your friends, let stories flow,
In this wild space, we steal the show.
Galaxies dance in jello cups,
As we toast to the stellar ups.

Cheers to the night, let's drink it right!
With playful stars, we'll shine so bright.
In laughter mixed with stardust cheer,
Every sip brings the cosmos near.

Illuminating the Void

In the void, we find our fun,
A black hole's laugh has just begun.
Banter like asteroids, bouncing free,
Space hiccups echo, oh can't you see?

Nebulae froth in a fizzy brew,
Counting the stars, just me and you.
Galactic gigs, under moonlit beams,
Life's a wild ride, in cosmic dreams.

Float through laughter, trails of light,
Mix up the punch, it's outta sight!
Planets collide in a game we play,
Jovial spirits, come out and sway.

As meteors streak in a wink-up glance,
Join the dance, take a chance!
In this void, with cosmic noise,
We spin the night with endless joys.

Secrets in the Starlight

Whispers of starlight, secrets unfold,
In a bubbly punch, adventures bold.
Winking stars throw a party spree,
Join us now, just you and me.

Galaxies giggle, as we poke fun,
Microphones made from spoons, let's run!
Punchy punchlines, slapstick style,
We'll shine and sparkle, mile after mile.

Cosmic jokes, light-years away,
Tickling your fancy, night and day.
With every chortle, the cosmos beams,
Planetary punch is bursting at the seams.

Under the glow of shimmering skies,
Where laughter echoes and mischief lies.
Let's toast to secrets, bright as they seem,
In this universe, we'll always dream.

Glistening Insights of the Infinite

Peeking at vibes, the infinite calls,
In a glass of sparkle, wonder enthralls.
Galactic glints, like glittering fish,
Every sip opens a cosmic wish.

Twinkling more than just bright stars,
We sip the tales from wine-filled jars.
Quirky planets do jumps and flips,
As we share stories and playful quips.

Infinite wisdom, served on the side,
In the company of friends, we take pride.
As shooting stars dash with delight,
Laughter rockets, soaring in flight.

So let's toast to mishaps and cheers,
In this vast cosmos, we'll shatter fears.
With glistening insights, let's celebrate,
In our silly world, we cooperate.

Secrets Beneath the Aurora

In the glow of the night, a secret sips,
Whispers float on cosmic trips.
Aliens dance with quirky style,
Grinning wide, they stay awhile.

Glasses clink and laughter swells,
Extraterrestrial tales and spells.
Jupiter's moon is quite the host,
To Martians who love their cosmic toast.

Wormholes open, a twist of fate,
Time travelers join, it's never late.
With wormy jokes and cosmic bites,
Even black holes giggle at the sights.

So come grab a drink, stay for the spree,
Under the laughing nebulae.
Forget your worries, let out a cheer,
In this cosmic bar, there's nothing to fear.

Celestial Serenade

Beneath the Milky Way's grand sweep,
Aliens groove, but hop, don't leap.
Guitar riffs made of stardust strung,
While comets hum and quasars sung.

With every sip, a giggle spills,
Cosmic cocktails, our cheers, they thrill.
Ceres serves snacks, oh what a spread,
While Saturn's rings spin tunes in your head.

Martian rock stars, so out of tune,
Sing about the cosmic moon.
Dancing with the cosmic dust,
In our universe, we must, we must.

So shift your chair, let's all unite,
For a dazzling, wacky starlit night.
In this lounge where laughter flies,
Even the stars can't help but rise.

A Night in the Nebula

In a swirl of colors, laughter flows,
Comets shimmer, as the raucous goes.
Nebulae swirling, bright and bold,
With stories of mischief that must be told.

A purple drink, with sprinkles galore,
Aliens toast, and ask for more.
Galactic jokes that never tire,
In this fusion, we all conspire.

From Pluto's bites to Mars' warm cheese,
Tales of mischief bring us to our knees.
Black holes wink, they know it's a game,
With every sip, we feel the same.

So let's keep dancing, forget the clock,
While time and space gallantly mock.
In this night of spark and mad design,
We laugh, we sip, and share the wine.

Glittering Memories of Midnight

Starlit shadows, mischief so bright,
Space oddities dance through the night.
Those Martian girls with glittery flair,
    Ask the robots if they dare.

Saucers zoom in, a party galore,
And the couch is filled with snacks to score.
Cheers echo through the expanse of night,
    Leaving us giggling in pure delight.

A dance-off starts, engines roar,
With cosmic giants, who could ask for more?
The universe winks, secrets untold,
    As we create precious moments of gold.

With every laugh, our spirits ignite,
    In this memory of joyful flight.
So pour another round, let's celebrate,
In the shimmer of the midnight fate.

The Night's Hidden Crescendo

In a room where secrets bloom,
Stars giggle in the gloom,
Tapping feet on liquid light,
Dancing shadows take to flight.

Bubbling drinks with curious names,
As laughter plays its silly games,
Celestial pie served on a plate,
Who knew the moon could taste so great?

Charming tales of comets' tails,
The jukebox plays as the laughter sails,
A cosmic wink from a shooting star,
Twirling tipsy under Venus's spar.

As night wraps tight like a velvet glove,
Everyone's friends, there's plenty of love,
The hidden beats of joy resound,
In this quiet chaos, magic is found.

Interstellar Whispers

In whispers soft like stardust dreams,
Galaxies twinkle and make strange schemes,
A comet sneezes, and chaos ensues,
As aliens swap their outlandish shoes.

The drinks are purple, the jokes are bold,
Like cosmic glitter, they never grow old,
With winks from Mars and giggles from Pluto,
These space oddities steal every show.

Asteroid pizzas float through the air,
And moonbeams dangle from every chair,
Astrological karaoke under the stars,
As laughter echoes through cosmic bars.

So grab a friend, and lift a cheer,
To the wild fun that brings us here,
Where every night's a cosmic spin,
And the universe just invites you in!

The Cosmic Connection

Across the universe, laughter rings,
Where each star wears fancy bling,
A pie chart made of space-time cream,
Shakes shared with an interstellar meme.

Twinkling lights in a foamy cup,
Watching Martians dance and sup,
Bubbles merge with celestial sound,
Beneath the canopy where fun abounds.

Cosmic mischief, a playful tease,
Meteor showers bring to knees,
The punchlines fly like shooting stars,
Cracking jokes from Jupiter to Mars.

While black holes giggle and comets play,
We toast to worlds at the end of the day,
In this wild whirl of joy unbound,
The cosmic connection knows no ground.

Luminous Paths in the Sky

Underneath a blanket of glittering dreams,
Cosmic jesters plot brilliant schemes,
With laughter bubbling like a bright nebula,
And dancing sparks that will never fail ya.

A cosmic dance with friends so dear,
Jokes collide, and nothing's clear,
As starlit cocktails sip with glee,
Mixing joy with a dash of spree.

Pulsars thump to a wacky beat,
As every quirky soul finds their seat,
With celestial games that twist and bend,
The night's a canvas—just grab a friend.

In shimmering beams, the cosmos chats,
About aliens and their silly hats,
Here we laugh, in this glowing sphere,
Finding the joy that brings us near.

Liquid Light from Afar

In a bar at the edge of space,
They serve dreams with a funny face.
Martinis made of comet's tails,
And laughter echoes through the scales.

Space whales dance with cosmic glee,
While time fumbles like a clumsy bee.
The jukebox spins a quasar tune,
As aliens waltz beneath the moon.

With every sip, the stars all grin,
As gossip flows like liquid gin.
A bartender with a warm, bright grin,
Says, "The universe is wide, dive in!"

Floating chairs in neon glow,
Where shadows swish, and stardust flows.
A cosmic bar, so wild and free,
Where hiccups travel light-speed glee.

Beyond the Veil of Stars

Whispers swirl in the cosmic air,
Critters trade secrets with flair.
A tap-dancing comet steals the show,
With winks from moons, all aglow.

Beyond the veil, the jesters play,
With punchlines that light up the Milky Way.
They juggle meteors, drop in style,
Each laugh a supernova's smile.

Planets spin while sipping tea,
Swapping jokes like a cosmic spree.
The stars roll their eyes at the punning glow,
As cosmic jesters take a bow, you know?

A nebula wraps around with glee,
Cheering for 'who knows'? or 'that's me!'
In the laughter of light years, we reside,
In this interstellar joyride.

Melodies of the Universe's Heart

In a galaxy where humor flows,
Every note from the cosmos glows.
Silly symphonies of quirky stars,
Plucking laughter from dust-filled jars.

A moon hums a bouncing tune,
While asteroids groove with a cheeky swoon.
Pulsars thump like a big band beat,
As constellations sway their feet.

Dancing comets with tails so long,
Crooning ballads that feel so wrong.
Each twinkle adds a dash of fun,
As the Milky Way joins in the run.

So gather your friends in this cosmic bar,
Catch a laugh on the horizon's star.
For in the universe's hearty mirth,
Every giggle is a spark of birth.

Celestial Conversations Unveiled

In the dark, where stars confide,
Celestial chatter can't be denied.
A planet spills tea with a wink and smile,
While black holes joke about lost time, meanwhile.

Galaxies spin tales of woe,
While meteors share their latest show.
A rocket ship laughs, 'Are we lost?'
Stars reply, 'No, just a fun frost!'

Stardust sprinkled like fairy dust,
In this cosmic banter, we all trust.
Even supernovae crack a jest,
As light-years zip on a cosmic quest.

So sip your drink under moons aglow,
Join in the fun, let your laughter flow.
In the universe's grand chat soirée,
Every wit, a shining ballet.

Celestial Conversations

The stars are having quite the chat,
While planets laugh and dance like that.
They spill their drinks, cosmic confetti,
Whirling around, oh so petty.

A comet slides in with a cheesy grin,
Telling jokes about where it's been.
Laughter bubbles in the vacuum glow,
Even black holes can't say no!

They argue over who's the brightest ball,
While meteors shoot and giggle, enthralled.
Uranus can't take the roguish tease,
Rolling around like a cosmic breeze.

Bright nebulae slosh in shimmering hue,
Sipping starlight, with a cosmic crew.
Celestial friends with a splendid jest,
In this space tavern, they've been blessed!

Whispers of the Nightsky

Up above, the whispers fly,
Moonbeams giggle, oh me, oh my!
Asteroids gossip in a playful swirl,
While their dust turns into a twinkling pearl.

"Did you hear what Venus wore?"
"Neptune's been crashing the dance floor!"
Saturn spins tales of rings and flair,
Each planet sharing, without a care.

Comets swoosh past with a wink and nudge,
Shooting stars calling out, "Let's not judge!"
The nightsky's vibrant with jokes and jest,
In every shadow, humor's the guest.

Galaxies stretch like a cosmic grin,
Each whisper heralds where joy begins.
They toast to eons and fun from above,
Crafting laughter with stellar love.

Moonlit Gatherings

Under a winking lunar glow,
Gather round, it's quite the show!
Stars are chatting with cheeky sparks,
Time for jokes in this cosmic park.

The owls join in, hooting with glee,
As alien friends sip moonlit tea.
Gravity plays tricks, making them sway,
Laughing and sliding, what a display!

"Who ordered cheese on this meteor?"
"Oh, that's mine! Just a little more!"
Galactic giggles fill the night air,
Laughter echoing without a care.

And if a rocket should zoom on through,
They hop in step, join in the brew.
Moonlit gatherings, a comet's delight,
Spinning tales 'til the morning light!

Cosmic Elixirs

In a hidden nook of the Milky Way,
Cosmic bartenders serve dreams in a tray.
Nebula mix, they shake with flair,
Pouring bright colors beyond compare.

"Give me a splash of supernova zest!"
"Add some stardust for the very best!"
Planets slurp from shimmering glasses,
While meteor showers treat with passes.

Twinkling mocktails for every star,
"Cheers to the universe, near and far!"
With every sip, laughter flows wide,
As cosmic friends revel in pride.

Then comes a planet with a dizzy twirl,
"Is that the friend from another world?"
In this bar of dreams, where spirits soar,
Cosmic elixirs, forevermore!

Secrets Among the Stars

In a bar up high where comets dance,
There's a moonlight cocktail, take a chance.
The patrons are aliens, all dressed to thrill,
They sip on stardust, it's quite a chill.

A Martian's joke makes gravity sway,
While Saturn's rings jingle in disarray.
The sunbeam waiter spills cosmic tea,
Laughing at orbits, so wild and free.

Asteroids nod to the beat of the tunes,
As spaceships waltz 'neath mischievous moons.
A galaxy gossip, swirling with flair,
With black holes grinning, they lighten the air.

Here secrets are whispered, quite out of sight,
In galaxies bright, all giggles take flight.
So come take a seat and enjoy the ride,
At this cosmic tavern, let laughter be wide.

Celestial Spirits

In a tavern where star-tails flicker and gleam,
The drinks are made from a nebula's dream.
A cosmic bartender, with humor to spare,
Mixes up laughter and cosmic strawberry flair.

Sprites dance on tables, twirling about,
While space-time donuts leave customers stout.
A Jupiter giant shares tales with a grin,
Of black hole pranks and the mess they're in.

Quasars giggle as they sip glowing brew,
Comets join in, it's a wild view.
Spirits float by, dressed in moonbeam attire,
Each glass raised high, sparking cosmic fire.

Laughter erupts in this stellar retreat,
With everyone howling, it's quite the feat.
So toast to the cosmos and all it imparts,
In this whimsical realm, where fun never departs.

The Galaxy's Hidden Room

In a nook of the cosmos, a door creaks wide,
Where meteors mingle and dark matter hides.
The bouncer's a star with a sparkle and sway,
Letting in joy, keeping boredom at bay.

A little green fellow shows off his dance,
His moves like a satellite, spinning by chance.
With astrological jokes landing like meteors,
The laughter erupts like popcorn in stores.

Each table boasts quirks, from a nebula stew,
To cocktails that glimmer with shades of the blue.
The secret's out, and the vibes fill the room,
As starlit antics make the night bloom.

So join in the fun, it's a cosmic tease,
Where laughter ignites like a solar breeze.
In this hidden retreat, we're all a bit mad,
And joking with planets, oh, how it's rad!

Eclipsed Encounters

In a lively lounge where shadows take flight,
The drinks are eclipses, the mood's just right.
A shadowy figure with a wink, he spills,
Tales of adventures that give you the thrills.

Lunar lattes brew a surreal delight,
As comets collide in the heart of the night.
A galaxy dancer winks with a grin,
Enticing the stars to join in the spin.

The jokes are eclipsing with cosmic finesse,
As everyone giggles, the chaos a mess.
With humor so bright, it lights up the gloom,
In a stellar soirée, where laughter can bloom.

So raise up your glasses, let's toast to the skies,
In this pocket of laughter, where whimsy flies.
Here every encounter is eclipsed by sheer joy,
In the embrace of the cosmos, let's all be coy!

Radiance of Midnight Wanderlust

In a bar of twinkling lights, they toast,
With drinks invented by a lunar ghost.
The martinis sparkled, like the night sky,
And laughter echoed, oh my, oh my!

A cat in a tux steps on a shoe,
Sipping a cocktail, thinks it's fondue.
The starry patrons all cheer and clash,
As confetti falls in a glittery splash.

Dancing on tables, their toes getting sore,
An alien band plays, what a wild score!
The moon winks down with a cheeky grin,
While folks spin wildly, let the fun begin!

At the stroke of two, a comet zooms by,
An impromptu dance-off, who's this shy guy?
In the glow of this cosmic, zany spree,
They toast to the night, just pure jubilee!

Explorations in Stellar Spirit

At a bar where the comets gossip and sway,
Jupiters dance, in a most clumsy display.
Martian waiters juggle snacks with great flair,
Saturn's rings spin, oh, what a strange affair!

A drink called 'Moonlight Mischief' they sip,
Giggling at aliens who're missing a trip.
A green one croons, making hearts all aflutter,
While a shy star whispers, 'That's not my butter!'

Do they serve peanuts or meteors here?
A Martian says, 'Only if you bring beer!'
Each laugh a sparkle, each toast a delight,
In this place where the cosmos feels just right.

As the clock strikes, a black hole appears,
Swallowing socks, and a few shifty beers.
Yet all are delighted, in whimsical cheer,
For the magic of laughter can conquer all fear!

A Night of Galactic Wonders

Under a canopy of shimmering lights,
A zebra-striped moon hosts fantastic sights.
Each hiccup a supernova, bursting with joy,
As particle pals tease the princely young boy.

In the corner, a robot sings off-key,
While space cows compete in a line dance spree.
The drinks are wild, with flavors unknown,
What is this? Cosmic fruit? Or fizz from a bone?

A vacuum cleaner glides with fantastic ease,
Sucking up troubles like dust on a breeze.
Neon donuts float high, like dreams in the air,
And everyone's chuckling, without a care.

At the stroke of three, with starry-eyed glee,
They hold hands together, as one cosmic tree.
The wonders of night, oh what a great plan,
Where the universe winks at the best of the clan!

Dances of the Ether

In a space lounge where the glowworms meet,
Not a chair in sight, just a bubbling treat.
A comet-shaped cake glides past with a grin,
While starfish skitter about in a spin.

A disco ball made from stardust and beams,
Reflects laughter louder than wildest of dreams.
A squirrel in moon boots messes up the show,
But everyone cheers, 'Hey, let it flow!'

Dancing through nebulae, they twirl and glide,
Mistaking a potted plant for a guide.
Each step an adventure, each laugh a delight,
As the milky way winks, declaring the night.

With a clink of their glasses, they toast once more,
To these gatherings of wits, utmost galore!
In this crazy expanse, they'll always believe,
That a night filled with joy is what they shall weave!

The Cosmic Cocktail

In a glass of dreams, galaxies swirl,
With a twist of fate and a twist of pearl.
A bartender winks, with a starry grin,
Mixing up laughter, let the night begin.

Neon drinks float, in orbit they dance,
Planets collide, with a spaced-out chance.
Sipping on joy, with a side of mirth,
Cosmic giggles bounce around the Earth.

Asteroids on ice, with a dash of glee,
Jupiter smiles, says, "Join me for tea!"
Swirling in bliss, beyond the moon's light,
Where hiccups are stardust, and everything's bright.

So raise your glass, let the stars ignite,
In this cosmic jamboree, all wrong feels right.
As we toast to the skies, and the friends we meet,
In this galactic bar, where laughter's the treat.

Nightfall at the Edge of Infinity

As twilight whispers, the cosmos sprawls,
With shimmery wonders and jubilant calls.
Hidden behind comets, the laughter erupts,
Dancing with shadows, where chaos corrupts.

Celestial critters prance on the floor,
With wobbly legs, they ask for more.
Shooting stars giggle as they flip and slide,
While black holes chuckle at the things we hide.

In this vibrant lounge, nebulae stretch,
Sipping on stories that time cannot fetch.
Each wink from a moonbeam, a playful tease,
Nightfall's a party, where worries freeze.

So grab a friend and gaze up high,
At the edge of infinity, where spirits fly.
With laughter like constellations that gleam,
We chase our wishes, and drift into dreams.

Chasing Shooting Stars

In the velvet sky, we chase the trails,
Of twinkling wishes and cosmic tales.
With popcorn comets, we make our aim,
Laughter erupts like a shooting flame.

Darting through time, the cosmos plays,
Navigating spaces in funny ways.
Stars have a sense of humor, it seems,
Their giggles echo in our wild dreams.

We step on light beams, with shoes made of fun,
Greet whirling galaxies, one by one.
A universe packed with a whimsical beat,
As we scamper to catch what slips through our feet.

So, wish on the trails that dance in the night,
Chase after joy, and hold on tight.
With a heart full of cheer and eyes open wide,
Together we'll soar, on this cosmic ride.

The Luminescent Gathering

When dusk falls down, the lumens ignite,
Gathering sparks, oh what a sight!
With vibrant tales in a glowing haze,
We dance in delight through the starlit maze.

Glimmers and giggles, interstellar cheer,
Chatting with meteors, who come near.
Flickering whispers of stories untold,
As laughter ignites in the cosmic fold.

A lounge filled with quirks, from which we sip,
Glows in the dark, on this wild trip.
The orbs of merriment bounce off the walls,
Beneath the celestial, where laughter enthralls.

So join the assembly, raise a bright glass,
In the flickering flames as moments pass.
With friends all around, and stardust to share,
This luminescent gathering, beyond compare.

The Radiant Sanctuary

In a room where laughter swirls,
And cosmic jokes unfurl,
We toast to stars and wine,
As dreams and giggles intertwine.

Beneath the twinkling lights we sway,
Dancing in a playful way,
With martinis that moonwalk,
And echoes of jokes that softly talk.

A cat in a top hat makes a toast,
To galaxies and giggles, we love the most,
While comets take their silly leap,
In a sanctuary where secrets keep.

So let the mirthful moments gleam,
As we share our wildest dream,
For here in this radiant delight,
We own the laughter of the night.

Midnight Muses

The clock strikes twelve, the fun begins,
With stories spun and playful sins,
We swirl in tales both wild and free,
While sipping on stardust-infused tea.

A jester twirls with a cosmic wand,
Making galaxies of mischief respond,
While poets stumble on their rhymes,
Claiming they're from other times.

In a waltz of whims and merry chance,
We laugh and jig in a silly dance,
Where planets giggle in delight,
And nightbirds chorus through the night.

Let's toast to quirks and cosmic tales,
As laughter spills like twinkling trails,
For in this midnight mirthful haze,
We find the joy of endless days.

Cosmic Revelry

With confetti of cosmos, we start the show,
As nebulae pirouette and glow,
In a revelry that's bright and bold,
Where tales of stardust glitter like gold.

A comet crashed but that's just fate,
We laugh it off, it's never too late,
With punchlines tossed like meteorites,
As space-time bends in our starry nights.

The DJ's spinning solar flares,
While laughter lightens all our cares,
As we groove among the starry cheer,
In a cosmic gathering year after year.

Raise your glasses, let's cheers with glee,
To the universe, and its playful spree,
For in this dance of joy and play,
We'll laugh until the break of day.

A Sip of the Universe

Pour a glass of cosmic cheer,
With bubbles of laughter, let's all steer,
To a place where whimsies thrive,
And giggles keep the night alive.

The stars, they wink, they stick their tongues,
While we toast to mischief and tangled lungs,
With cocktails that shimmer and shine,
We sip the universe, feeling divine.

The moon's our bartender, a crafty soul,
Mixing absurdities in a playful bowl,
As we chuckle through whims and dreams,
And dance through the night in sparkly beams.

So take a gulp of this starry delight,
With every sip, the future feels bright,
For here in this cosmic celebration,
We find our laughter's true foundation.

The Astral Soirée

In a glow that's quite surreal,
Dancing lights and cosmic zeal,
A rabbit in a shimmering coat,
Sips starlight from an old pink boat.

The moon wears shades; it's quite a sight,
Jiving with comets, feeling light,
While aliens serve cosmic tea,
With biscuits made of galaxy.

A floor of clouds, a sky of dreams,
Everyone laughs; nothing's as it seems,
With meteorites as party snacks,
We groove and jive, no looking back!

In this space of whipped up fun,
Where gravity's lost and puns weigh a ton,
The night's a comet, a merry chase,
As laughter echoes through this place.

Secrets of the Silver Sky

Whispers float on lunar beams,
Chasing shadows of silly dreams,
A group of owls in bow ties grin,
Plotting a heist on the starry spin.

The drinks are brewed from fallen mist,
And constellations can't resist,
A salad tossed with asteroid bits,
Sparks rocket laughter; how it flits!

Aliens croon in perfect tune,
Humming soft to the light of the moon,
With jokes that send the planets whirling,
As cosmic jokes leave others twirling.

In this realm of quirky glee,
Even the dark holes dance with spree,
Secrets shared in a cheeky blink,
Cosmic chuckles spill over the brink.

Twilight's Hidden Retreat

Behind the veil of evening's glow,
A secret nook where jesters go,
With velvet cupcakes and cosmic pies,
And punch that tickles—oh, what a surprise!

Chairs of clouds with legs that jive,
Inviting all to come alive,
Where fireflies tell tales absurd,
And giggles tumble, barely heard.

A gnome plays chess with starry bets,
While fairies trade their sparkly sets,
A disco ball made out of sun,
Keeps the rhythm, oh, what fun!

In this niche of joyful cheer,
It's clear that nonsense reigns here,
As twilight sparkles, laughter — a treat,
Everyone dancing on fluffy feet.

Nocturnal Revelations

Beneath the wide and winked-out beams,
The night uncovers playful schemes,
With jokes tossed high like shooting stars,
And laughter shared among the czars.

A walrus sings in silver shoes,
With tunes that make the stars confuse,
While pin-up bats spin 'round the floor,
Inviting all for just one more!

Nebulae spice up martini shakers,
As owls dance with intergalactic bakers,
The cosmos giggles at the sight,
Of every twist beneath the light.

In this gala of moonlit grace,
Everyone tumbles in this embrace,
With each revelation spun anew,
The night's a stage for dreams to pursue.

Gravity's Whisper

In the bar where comets spin,
A cocktail of dreams begins.
Nebulae serve gin on the rocks,
While asteroids dance in their socks.

Jupiter's clown with a giant hat,
Tells jokes that make you go splat!
Laughing stars join in the ruckus,
As Saturn's rings play the tuba for us.

Time flows like a wobbly drink,
As black holes pull you to the brink.
Planets wobble on their feet,
Grooving to an interstellar beat.

So raise a glass to the wild night,
As meteors flash in delight.
In the light of a million fires,
We dance as gravity conspires!

Lights Beyond the Horizon

Underneath the twinkling glow,
Quasars put on quite a show.
The Milky Way's a party zone,
Where laughter echoes, seeds are sown.

Aliens with top hats and tails,
Tell the best of all the tales.
They giggle and sip on stardust brew,
While multi-colored fish float through.

A cosmic band strikes up a tune,
Comets chirp like a cartoon.
The universe hums with delight,
As black holes waltz in the moonlight.

Join the fun on this wild ride,
As laughter swells like the tide.
There's no frown, just cosmic cheer,
In this place, there's naught to fear.

Whispers of Cosmic Laughter

In a galaxy where jesters play,
The cosmos chuckles the night away.
Stars twinkle with mischievous glee,
As the universe spills its tea.

A rocket ship race with a slip and slide,
Gravity forgot, we take a ride!
With meteors flinging silly confetti,
The laughter rolls—oh, isn't it petty?

Cosmic beings in sparkling attire,
Share puns that spark a cosmic fire.
The planets all giggle, how absurd!
Together, the laughter's the loudest word!

So sip your drink, let worries cease,
In this atmosphere, find your peace.
The echoes of joy ring through the night,
As stardust flutters in pure delight!

Celestial Soiree

At the edge of the astral floor,
The stars have opened the door.
Neon lights in the void gleam,
As we toast to the wildest dream.

With Martians juggling cosmic pies,
And Saturn's rings in flashy ties.
The cosmos wraps us in its glow,
As we dance in the cosmic show.

Milky Way drinks, bubbly and bright,
As we sway under ethereal light.
Galactic jokes float through the air,
Who knew space could be this rare?

So laugh it up, let spirits soar,
In the universe's vibrant core.
With a wink, the night hops along,
In a crazy cosmic sing-along!

Midnight in the Cosmic Cafe

In a diner where the stars conspire,
A waiter serves up solar fire.
The coffee's brewed from comets' trails,
And pancakes float like lunar gales.

Aliens toast with cosmic cheer,
While asteroids dance, not a single fear.
A cosmic jukebox plays a tune,
With melodies plucked from the giant moon.

UFOs park like they own the place,
Swinging around with style and grace.
They order martinis with a twist,
And laugh so hard, they can't resist.

As midnight strikes, the lights all blink,
And gravity's lost in a splash of pink.
With every sip, the stars align,
In this wild cafe, everything's fine.

Cosmic Dreams and Drinks

Underneath a glittering dome,
We sip on dreams and call it home.
With cosmic cocktails, none too plain,
Each sip can make you sing in vain.

A purple drink gives you wings to fly,
While chatting it up with a witty pye.
Galactic snacks that tickle the mind,
As we toast to things we're yet to find.

A little gnome drops by for a chat,
He spills his drink, 'Oh, where's my hat?'
The laughter erupts, the joy's in the air,
In space-time's grasp, we've no single care.

The rockets hum a jazzy tune,
While planets twirl like a little spoon.
In swirling lights our dreams would float,
One sip, one laugh—oh, who needs a boat?

The Velvet Night Unfolds

In velvet shadows, laughter spills,
With shooting stars and cosmic thrills.
We sip on joy from jeweled cups,
Where every clink brings laughter up.

A creature's tale, a jolly sight,
With tentacle arms, it twirls with delight.
It juggles moons and winks an eye,
Two cosmic cheers soar to the sky.

Neon dreams on every wall,
While echoes of joy in ribbons fall.
A game of chance, the stakes are low,
We laugh as meteors put on a show.

With every sip, the night unfurls,
Enchanted spins like dancing pearls.
This cosmic gala will never cease,
In playful dreams, we find our peace.

Beyond the Veil of Night

Past the edges where comets race,
In a realm where troubles erase.
We gather near the cosmic shore,
With drinks that sparkle and tales galore.

A wink from Mars, a nod from Mars,
As we toast to dreams with candy bars.
The stars giggle, twinkling bright,
Welcoming all to the playful night.

A moonlit shuffle, a nimble dance,
Where shadows play and dreamers prance.
We sip on tunes, both sweet and sour,
In this whimsical, timeless hour.

With every sip, we glide and sway,
And party like it's always play.
In a universe where fun takes flight,
We celebrate life beyond the night.

Stories from the Celestial Chamber

In a bar made of moonlight, they dance with glee,
Martians sip cocktails, while Venus twirls free.
Jupiters laugh, tossing peanuts quite high,
And Saturn's ring tips a drink from the sky.

A comet walks in, wearing shades and a grin,
He orders a smoothie, his fruit much too thin.
Asteroids giggle, they roll just for fun,
In this cosmic pub, there's always a pun.

Neptune's on stage, cracking jokes with a flair,
While aliens chuckle, their green hands in the air.
Black holes in the corner, they're sharing old tales,
Of cosmic adventures and interstellar fails.

So raise up a glass, toast the night without shame,
For the universe sparkles, what a wild game!
Stories of laughter, they echo and swell,
In the chamber of stars, where we laugh and dwell.

Starlit Conversations

Over drinks made of starlight, we stumble and cheer,
Talking of planets and what we all fear.
"Do black holes really suck?!" a Martian will shout,
While a Jupiter jester spins tales of doubt.

Twinkle-toed comets compete with their charms,
As they navigate space with their dance and their arms.
"Let's start a band!" cries a bold little moon,
And the crowd bursts with laughter to an astral tune.

A nebula winks, penning jokes in the fog,
While meteors flash in the laughter and smog.
We sip on our cocktails, a mix of the skies,
With thoughts on our drink choices, and colorful pies.

So join the conversation, let your cosmos spin,
For every laugh shared is a celestial win.
In this starlit retreat, where the wild giggles bloom,
The universe sparkles in this cosmic room.

Whimsy of the Wandering Planets

A wandering Titan tripped over a star,
With giggles erupting from near and from far.
Mars spilled his drink on a comet so fast,
Creating a splash that still lingers at last.

Sunshine and moonbeams, they dance on the floor,
While clever little Saturn shows off her decor.
"Celestial cupcakes!" a polka-dot sun,
Brings laughter and sugar, oh what a fun run!

While Pluto plays cards with a sly little grin,
He bets all his moons, claiming it's all in.
Laughter erupts from the Jovian crowd,
As he flips over cards, proud and so loud.

In the night sky's embrace, the planets collide,
With whimsy and wonder, they all take a ride.
Raise glasses to journeys where friendship's no end,
In the whimsical worlds where the galaxies blend.

A Toast to Astral Wanderers

Here's to the travelers of cosmic delight,
Who dance in the shadows of shimmering light.
With space hats and giggles, they frolic around,
In this playful escape where joy knows no bound.

The starry-eyed wanderers toast with a grin,
Poking fun at the planets, where chaos begins.
"Oh look, there's a dwarf!" cries a voice from the dark,
As laughter erupts like a cosmic spark.

Galaxies swirl, creating polka-dot schemes,
While starlings in groups spin their whimsical dreams.
They share silly stories, adventures so bright,
In a toast to the wonders that light up the night.

So clink those fine glasses, let the starlight make way,
For the laughter and joy that will always replay.
In this universe crowded, yet oh-so-unique,
Here's to the travelers, so vibrant and cheek!

Tales from the Astral Lounge

In the corner, sparkly lights,
A cat in shades, counting sights.
He sips a drink, purple and bold,
Telling tales of planets and gold.

Aliens dance with wobbly grace,
One tripped and fell, what a place!
They giggle like stars in the black,
And bounce right back, ready to crack.

A wise old comet sings a tune,
Waltzing with a bright green balloon.
The moon rolls its eyes, swaying tight,
For what a show, what a night!

So grab a drink, let laughter flow,
In this wild spot where weird folks go.
With asteroids hula-hooping around,
The fun's eternal, laughter unbound.

Moonlit Rhapsody

Underneath a cheese-like moon,
Frogs croak a most silly tune.
Worms wear top hats, tiny and spry,
As fireflies buzz, oh my, oh my!

A snail in a jacket tells bad jokes,
While giggling grasshoppers join the folks.
They tap their feet, keep time with ease,
In the vernal night, they aim to please.

Galactic drinks with fizz and pop,
A glimmering grape that won't stop.
Laughter rings like shooting stars,
In this wild bar, with a range of avatars.

So dance with twinkling, lovely glee,
In a shimmery world where all are free.
The night is whacky, and oh, so bright,
Join the moonlit fun, till morning light!

The Celestial Cabaret

In a room of colors, bold and bright,
Comets perform with all their might.
A starry jester juggles dreams,
And laughter flows like bubbling streams.

Planets play cards, stakes very high,
While meteor showers fall from the sky.
A disco ball spins with a twinkle,
Celestial beings share a giggle.

A dancing pluto, wiggly and round,
Steals the show without making a sound.
While laser lights dance on the wall,
This oddball spot has a ball!

So sit back, relax, enjoy the flair,
With curious critters, all must beware!
In this cabaret, where merriment strays,
Find joy in the weird in the cosmic maze.

Fantasia of the Fireflies

Beneath the glow of twinkling lights,
Fireflies boogie in silly flights.
A moth in a bowtie spins in place,
With waves of uniqueness, full of grace.

Bumblebees buzz, wearing crowns of gold,
As butterflies flaunt colors bold.
A caterpillar joins, looking refined,
With dreams of a dance floor in his mind.

The frog hosts karaoke, a hit for sure,
With ribbits and croaks that one can't ignore.
A conga line forms, fluttering by,
Underneath the vast, enchanting sky.

So come one, come all, to the light parade,
Where every moment is perfectly made.
With laughter and fun, oh what a sight,
In this whimsical world of pure delight!

Nighttime Reveries

In a corner, a cat dons a hat,
With a twirl of its tail, it's quite the diplomat.
A mouse offers cheese, with a wink and a grin,
Sipping starlit cocktails, let the night begin.

A moonbeam slides in, tipsy and bold,
Juggling fireflies, stories unfold.
Whispers of laughter rise with the smoke,
As dreams dance around, each a quirky joke.

The shadows all sway, like they're in on the fun,
As crickets join in, serenading the sun.
A glowing confetti of twilight is tossed,
In this midnight fiesta, no moment is lost.

A toast to the odd, the strange, and the bright,
As we hiccup our wishes to the endless night.
Underneath the glitter, we spin and we dive,
In a whimsical whir, we're more than alive.

Constellation Chronicles

A squirrel in a waistcoat recounts the stars,
With tales of brave raccoons and their fancy cars.
The owls roll their eyes, sipping moonlit tea,
As the cosmos unfolds gossip, wild and free.

Meteors zoom past, like mischief in queues,
Dropping off secrets and mismatched shoes.
Galactic shenanigans twirl in our heads,
As we laugh with the echoes of long-ago threads.

A comet tries stand-up, but stumbles on clouds,
While starlit spectators hoot, "You're too loud!"
The asteroids kibitz, trading old tales,
As laughter echoes through the endless trails.

So raise your glass high to the stories we weave,
With humor and sparkles, it's hard to believe.
In this cosmic cabaret, come join the spree,
With celestial chuckles as bright as can be.

Flicker of the Infinite

A firefly winks from the tip of a leaf,
Making jokes about shadows, causing brief grief.
The stars all chime in with a giggle or two,
As the universe winks, and says, "How do you do?"

Jupiter's laughing, spilling his drink,
While Saturn's rings wobble, what do you think?
Meteor showers cast a glow on the floor,
And the sun takes a nap, but it snorts, "No more!"

In this grand absurdity, glee is a must,
As quirky adventures await in the dust.
The cosmos invites us to frolic and play,
Where each little giggle lights up the way.

So twirl with the night, let your spirit unwind,
With laughter as currency, leave woes behind.
For in this grand flicker, we toast to our fate,
In the cosmic comedy, we celebrate.

Dreams in a Glass

At the bar of the twilight, we sip on the night,
With umbrellas dancing, all colors in sight.
A dragonfly bartender serves giggles with flair,
As laughter bubbles up, filling the air.

Each sip is a story, a twist of the fate,
Where time is elastic, the hour is late.
A star struggles in, tripping over its shine,
Professing its love for the wobbling wine.

With neon galaxies swirling so bright,
All the wishes we drink, giving heart a light fight.
The comets chuckle, rolling on the floor,
As we toast in this realm where there's always more.

So raise your glass high and dance with delight,
In this cocktail of whimsy, our spirits take flight.
For dreams in our glasses, we all share the cheer,
In this jovial tavern, there's nothing to fear.

The Lounge of Lost Dreams

In the corner, a cat plays chess,
With a hat that's far too big, I confess.
A bird orders pie, then takes a stance,
Wings flapping wildly, it's a curious dance.

The drinks are all mixed by a juggling frog,
Who spills them while singing a comical slog.
Patrons in hats made of old pizza boxes,
Swap tales of their socks and their oddities' boxes.

A worm in a suit tells of space travel's flair,
His stories are wild, and yet, quite the scare.
The moon laughs loudly, blinking with glee,
As a ghost does the cha-cha, just wait and see.

In the glow of the lanterns, a pickle in pants,
Invites all the folks for a twirling chance.
With echoes of laughter that float on the breeze,
This lounge is a treasure, it's sure to please.

Tales Between the Tides

A fish in a tux offers tales of the sea,
While sand crabs conspire with glee to agree.
They sip on their cocktails, each one a delight,
Underneath the waves, in the glow of moonlight.

Seashells discuss fashion, with pearls in a row,
They rock to the rhythm of the undertow.
With giggles and whispers, they share tales of old,
Of octopuses dancing, and mermaids bold.

The jellyfish jive in a shimmering trance,
While dolphins join in with a bubbly dance.
A treasure chest opens to reveal a refrain,
Of fishy-backed stories that rain down like rain.

In that watery realm, where the quirky collide,
The laughter and joy turn the tide with pride.
Each wave tells a story, a fine little jest,
In the tales between tides, you'll find all the best.

Nebula's Hidden Tavern

In a cosmic corner, where starlings collide,
Lies a tavern of wonders, with friends side by side.
A robot sings songs of lost time and space,
While a comet tips drinks, a dazzling grace.

Planets stack chips in a game of pure luck,
And aliens chatter, "What's a good pluck?"
A nebula spills colors, paints laughter anew,
As they toast to the stars, and the joy that they brew.

Galaxies giggle at the puns in the air,
While shooting stars play hopscotch without a care.
A cyborg with flair serves up drinks on a tray,
Each sip full of joy, shooting worries away.

With whispers of comets that swirl in a tune,
The crowd dances wildly beneath a bright moon.
In this hidden tavern, the laughter won't cease,
For in the vast cosmos, there's always a piece.

Enchanted Echoes

In a grove where the fireflies gather and hum,
A fox tells a tale of a magical drum.
With echoes of laughter that float through the trees,
Each critter joins in with a whimsical tease.

The owls wear spectacles, reading the night,
While rabbits concoct brews that bubble just right.
A dance of the shadows, where giggles abound,
Creates jests in the roots, all around, all around.

The plants have their secrets, with petals that chat,
Sharing stories of mischief, "You won't believe that!"
As cicadas' rhythm sets the night's pace,
Each echo a memory, a warm, sweet embrace.

In this enchanted realm, where the silly reside,
The humor's infectious, you simply can't hide.
So come with your stories, and join in the fun,
In the laughter of echoes, together as one.

Constellation Confluences

In a bar where the stars align,
The bartender serves moonlight fine.
Comets slice through cocktails bright,
While aliens dance, what a sight!

Martians mix a fizzy brew,
Uranus orders something blue.
Jupiter laughs, it's quite a show,
With cosmic jokes, they steal the glow.

A telescope's the piano here,
Cosmic notes we all can hear.
Venus winks, it's cheeky fun,
While Saturn does a little run.

Polaris takes the floor in glee,
Glittering face, how bright must be!
The constellations join the trance,
In a swirling, starry dance!

Night Whisperers

Within the gloom, we sip and sway,
As fireflies join the cabaret.
A witty comet cracks a joke,
While the moon beams, and starlight croaks.

Laughter rolls like thunder's roar,
As we spill drinks on the floor.
The night owls hoot, they are our crew,
With quirky tales of skies so blue.

Black holes murmur secrets tight,
While galaxies shine through the night.
Jokes collide in sparkling air,
With each sip, we float without a care.

Swinging between the laughter's grace,
Through stardust trails, we find our place.
The cosmos gabs, with glee we toast,
To the night's fun, we cherish most!

The Celestial Afterglow

When the sun dips low, stars convene,
Creating mysteries, a fun-filled scene.
A nebula's twirl brings giggles near,
While black holes whisper, 'Come, have a beer!'

Galactic puns fly through the haze,
As Martian laughter crowns the days.
Cosmic hiccups rise to the sky,
With winks exchanged in by and by.

Asteroids stumble, trying to dance,
In the glow, they take their chance.
Meteor showers drop a beat,
While dancing quasars can't be beat!

The afterglow wraps us tight,
In the warmth of this cosmic night.
Toast to the stars, let spirits grow,
With humorous tales of the starlit show!

Concoctions of the Cosmos

In a laboratory spun from dreams,
Mixing potions in moonlight beams.
Galactic fizz and shooting stars,
A blend of laughter from afar.

Charming spirits, those cosmic whisks,
Stirring up a brew of risky twists.
With every sip, a wink and cheer,
The universe laughs, pulling us near.

Sip a nebula, taste the fun,
Where globes of ice turn into sun.
The recipes are wild and weird,
In this cosmic show, we all are steered!

From planetary steam to solar punch,
Each drink's a giggle, every crunch.
Laughing until the starlight's bright,
In concoctions pure, we find our light!

www.ingramcontent.com/pod-product-compliance
Lightning Source LLC
Chambersburg PA
CBHW051633160426
43209CB00004B/623